Life in the UK Test Exam Book
2022

Ashuk Miah

This edition published in the United Kingdom in 2022 by The Choir Press

ISBN 978-1-78963-332-0

Disclaimer: The author and publisher have made every effort to ensure that the information in this book is correct at the time of publication. However, the author and publisher do not assume and hereby disclaim any liability to any party for any loss, damage, or disruption caused by errors or omissions, whether such errors or omissions result from negligence, accident, or any other cause. The questions and answers in this book are examples of questions that candidates could encounter and actual exam questions may vary in style and scope.

Contents

Section 1   1
Practice Test 1: British History   3
Practice Test 2: British History   6
Practice Test 3: British History   10
Practice Test 4: British History   13
Practice Test 5: British History   16
Answers   20

Section 2   23
Practice Test 1: British Politics and Principles   25
Practice Test 2: British Politics and Principles   29
Practice Test 3: British Politics and Principles   32
Practice Test 4: British Politics and Principles   35
Practice Test 5: British Politics and Principles   38
Answers   42

Section 3   45
Practice Test 1: British Culture and Entertainment   47
Practice Test 2: British Culture and Entertainment   50
Practice Test 3: British Culture and Entertainment   53
Practice Test 4: British Culture and Entertainment   57
Answers   60

Contents

Section 4   63

Practice Test 1: British Law   65
Practice Test 2: British Law   68
Practice Test 3: British Law   72
Answers   75

Section 5   77

Practice Test 1: British Geography and National Information   79
Practice Test 2: British Geography and National Information   82
Answers   86

Section 6   87

Practice Test 1: Religion, Traditions and Special Dates   89
Practice Test 2: Religion, Traditions and Special Dates   93
Answers   97

About the author

This easy to use book has been developed to advise and guide candidates to pass the *Life in the UK Test* examination.

Ashuk Miah is an immigration lawyer who has been advising on immigration law for almost 20 years and has been involved in delivering ESOL lessons to students since it became a requirement by the UK Border Agency from 2009.

He is one of a few selected immigration lawyers who are chosen to explain the complexities of immigration rules to television audiences in the United Kingdom, Europe and Central America on a regular basis. He regularly appears on live TV shows where he answers questions from viewers from all over the world.

Ashuk Miah has run an approved ESOL Centre since 2009 and is therefore familiar with all the teaching materials and the kind of questions candidates can expect to encounter in the *Life in the UK* test examination. This book is the result of his extensive research to help students pass the exam.

My Promise to you

My aim is to provide continuous advice, support and teaching materials for the Life in the UK test to all our readers and we look forward to having a professional relationship with our readers for many years to come.

Section 1
British History

	page
Practice Test 1	3
Practice Test 2	6
Practice Test 3	10
Practice Test 4	13
Practice Test 5	16
Answers	20

British History
Practice Test 1

Question 1 Which of the following statements is correct?
A   In 1588 the English defeated a Spanish invasion fleet of ships
B   In 1588 the English defeated a German invasion fleet of bomber planes

Question 2 Which TWO are English Civil War battles?
A   Waterloo
B   Marston Moor
C   Hastings
D   Naseby

Question 3 Which of the following statements is correct?
A   Mary, Queen of Scots was unrelated to Queen Elizabeth I
B   Mary, Queen of Scots was a cousin of Queen Elizabeth I

Question 4 Which of the following statements is correct?
A   'The Divine Right of Kings' meant that the English king should rule the world
B   'The Divine Right of Kings' meant that the king was appointed by God

Question 5 What important event happened in England in 1066?
A   The Romans left England
B   The building of the Offa Dyke
C   The Norman Invasion
D   The Battle of Bannockburn

Question 6 Which of the following statements is correct?
A   Elizabeth I handled Parliament poorly during her reign
B   Elizabeth I had very good relations with Parliament

Question 7   Which TWO were associated with King Charles I and Parliament during the English Civil War?

A   Tories
B   Roundheads
C   Cavaliers
D   Luddites

Question 8   Is the statement below TRUE or FALSE?
   'The Restoration' refers to the re-establishment of Catholicism as the official Church in the 17th century

Question 9   Why was the Magna Carta important?

A   It gave all men more rights
B   It limited the power of the monarch
C   It established a new system of free education
D   It gave women legal rights

Question 10   Which of the following statements is correct?

A   The Industrial Revolution was the rapid development of industry in the 18th and 19th centuries
B   The Industrial Revolution introduced changes in the education system in the 1980s

Question 11   Is the statement below TRUE or FALSE?
   In 1805 at the Battle of Trafalgar, Admiral Nelson defeated the German fleet

Question 12   Is the statement below TRUE or FALSE?
   Wales united with England during the reign of Henry VIII

Question 13   Which of the following statements is correct?

A   Charles, king of Scotland, was restored as King Charles II of England in 1660
B   Bonnie Prince Charlie became King Charles II of England in 1660

Question 14   What were 'The Troubles' about?

A   Independence for Wales
B   Disagreement over Ireland becoming one country
C   Independence for Scotland
D   Setting up an English Parliament

Question 15   Which TWO fought in wars against Napoleon?
A   Margaret Thatcher
B   Horatio Nelson
C   Tony Blair
D   The Duke of Wellington

Question 16   Which of the following statements is correct?
A   In the 18th century two political groups emerged, the Whigs and the Tories
B   In the 18th Century two political groups emerged, the Conservatives and the Liberals

Question 17   In 1348 a third of the populations of England, Wales and Scotland died as a result of which plague?
A   The Pink Death
B   The White Death
C   The Red Death
D   The Black Death

Question 18   For which TWO reasons is Henry VIII remembered?
A   Fighting
B   Married six times
C   Broke away from the Church of Rome
D   Drinking too much alcohol

Question 19   Is the statement below TRUE or FALSE?
When Queen Anne died, a German, George of Hanover, became the next King of England

Question 20   Which of the following is a famous Stone Age site in the UK?
A   London Eye
B   Buckingham Palace
C   Stonehenge
D   Windsor Castle

British History
Practice Test 2

Question 1   Textile and engineering firms recruited workers from which TWO countries after the Second World War?
A   North America
B   Canada
C   India
D   Pakistan

Question 2   Which of the following statements is correct?
A   The 'plantation' settlements in Ireland during the 17th century led to Protestant farmers replacing Catholic landowners
B   The 'plantation' settlements in Ireland during the17th century led to Catholic farmers replacing Protestant landowners

Question 3   Which language was spoken by people during the Iron Age?
A   Latin
B   Celtic
C   Greek
D   Anglo-Saxon

Question 4   Which TWO records tell us about England during the time of William I?
A   Domesday Book
B   Diary of Samuel Pepys
C   Magna Carta
D   Bayeux Tapestry

Question 5   Which form of religion developed as a result of the Reformation?
A   Catholicism
B   Protestantism
C   Islam
D   Hinduism

Question 6   Is the statement below TRUE or FALSE?
A public vote in 2002 decided that Winston Churchill was the Greatest Briton of all time

Question 7   Why was the Habeas Corpus Act of 1679 so important?
A   It ensured no person could be held unlawfully
B   It allowed people to bury the dead where they wished
C   It ensured that those who died could only be buried by their own family
D   It ended capital punishment in England

Question 8   Which TWO wars was England involved in during the Middle Ages?
A   Crimean
B   Crusades
C   Hundred Years War
D   Peninsular

Question 9   Which of the following statements is correct?
A   During Queen Elizabeth I's reign, English settlers began to colonise New Zealand
B   During Queen Elizabeth I's reign, English settlers began to colonise the eastern coast of North America

Question 10   Which queen is remembered for her rebellion against the Romans?
A   Elizabeth
B   Boudicca
C   Victoria
D   Anne

Question 11   Is the statement below TRUE or FALSE?
The jet engine and radar were developed in Britain in 1830s

Question 12 What did St Augustine and St Columba do during the Anglo-Saxon period?

A   They invented new fighting techniques

B   They were leaders of an uprising in Wales

C   They were early Christian missionaries

D   They were courageous warriors

Question 13 Which of the following statements is correct?

A   The Industrial Revolution is the name given to the rapid development of industry in Britain in the 20th century

B   The Industrial Revolution is the name given to the rapid development of industry that began in the 18th century

Question 14 Is the statement below TRUE or FALSE?

During the 18th century, radical new ideas about politics, philosophy and science were developed, called 'the Enlightenment'

Question 15 Which of the following statements is correct?

A   The first professional UK football clubs were formed in the late 19th century

B   The first professional UK football clubs were formed in 1066

Question 16 What were TWO important aspects of the Reform Act of 1832?

A   It decreased the power of the monarch

B   It increased the number of people who could vote

C   It abolished rotten boroughs

D   It gave women the right to work

Question 17 For approximately how many years did the Romans stay in this country?

A   200 years

B   100 years

C   400 years

D   600 years

Question 18 Is the statement below TRUE or FALSE?

The 'Swinging Sixties' is associated with the 1980s

Question **19**   Where did the Vikings come from?
A   Germany and Italy
B   Belgium and Sweden
C   Denmark and Norway
D   France and Luxemburg

Question **20**   Which of the following statements is correct?
A   The Reform Act of 1832 increased the number of electors
B   The Reform Act of 1832 increased the power of the House of Commons

British History
Practice Test 3

Question 1   Is the statement below TRUE or FALSE?
In 1588 the English fleet defeated a large French fleet of ships that intended to land an army in England

Question 2   Who was given the title of Lord Protector in the 17th century?
A   King Charles II
B   Samuel Pepys
C   Oliver Cromell
D   Isaac Newton

Question 3   Is the statement below TRUE or FALSE?
'We shall fight them on the beaches' is a famous quote from a speech by the Queen Elizabeth I about the Spanish Armada

Question 4   Which of the following statements is correct?
A   In 1776 some American colonies declared their independence from Britain
B   American colonists were eventually defeated by the British

Question 5   When was the last successful invasion of England?
A   1066
B   1415
C   1642
D   1950

Question 6   Is the statement below TRUE or FALSE?
John Constable (1776–1837) founded the modern police force in England

Question 7   Which TWO are 20th-century British discoveries or inventions?
A   Hovercraft
B   Rockets
C   Penicillin
D   Computers

Question 8   Which of the following statements is correct?
A   During the First World War Winston Churchill was the British Prime Minister
B   During the Second World War Winston Churchill was the British Prime Minister

Question 9   Who were the 'suffragettes'?
A   Women who left the UK to live in Asia
B   Women who campaigned for women's votes
C   Women who chose to be single
D   Women who stayed at home to raise a family

Question 10   Which TWO are 20th-century British discoveries or inventions?
A   Cloning a mammal
B   Cash machines (ATMs)
C   Mobile phones
D   Computers

Question 11   Which Scottish king defeated the English at the Battle of Bannockburn in 1314?
A   William Wallace
B   Robert the Bruce
C   Malcom
D   Andrew

Question 12   Is the statement below TRUE or FALSE?
   During the Victorian period the British Empire became the largest empire the world has ever seen

Question 13   Is the statement below TRUE or FALSE?
   Before 1215 there were no laws to limit the power of the king of England

Question 14 Which TWO of the following were major welfare changes introduced from **1945** to **1950**?

A   National Health Service (NHS)
B   State retirement pension
C   Employment Rights
D   A social security system for all

Question 15 Which of the following statements is correct?

A   The 'Swinging Sixties' was a period of religious change
B   The 'Swinging Sixties' was a period of social change

Question 16 Which of the following statements is correct?

A   The Reform Act of 1832 decreased the number of voters
B   The Reform Act 1832 increased the number of voters

Question 17 Is the statement below TRUE or FALSE?

In 1921 a treaty gave independence to the South of Ireland

Question 18 Which TWO were introduced before the First World War **(1914)**?

A   National Health Service (NHS)
B   Child Benefit payments
C   State retirement pension
D   Free school meals

Question 19 Which of the following statements is correct?

A   The Battle of Britain in 1940 was fought at sea
B   The Battle of Britain in 1940 was fought in the skies

Question 20 Which of the following statements is correct?

A   The Roman army left England after 200 years to defend other parts of their Empire
B   The Roman army left England after 400 years to defend other parts of their Empire

British History
Practice Test 4

Question 1 Is the statement below TRUE or FALSE?
The Civil War between Henry VIII and Parliament in the mid-17th century led to Oliver Cromwell becoming king of England

Question 2 Is the statement below TRUE or FALSE?
In the 1830s and 1840s a group called the Chartists campaigned for reform to the voting system

Question 3 During the 'Great Depression' of the 1930s, which TWO major new industries developed?
A Shipbuilding
B Coal mining
C Automobile
D Aviation

Question 4 The Bill of Rights of 1689 limited whose powers?
A The king
B The police
C The judiciary
D The Church

Question 5 Is the statement below TRUE or FALSE?
In 1707 the kingdoms of England and Scotland were united

Question 6 Which of the following statements is correct?
A The Anglo-Saxon kingdoms in England were united under King Alfred the Great
B The Anglo-Saxon kingdoms were united under King George III

Question 7   Which of the following statements is correct?
A   Hadrian's Wall was built on the orders of the Roman Emperor Hadrian
B   Hadrian's Wall was built by the Picts (ancestors of the Scottish people) to keep out the Romans

Question 8   Which TWO famous London buildings are built in the 19th-century 'gothic' style?
A   The Shard
B   The Houses of Parliament
C   St Pancras Station
D   Buckingham Palace

Question 9   Is the statement below TRUE or FALSE?
King Henry VIII created the Church of England when the Pope refused to grant him a divorce

Question 10   Which TWO developments are associated with the 'Swinging Sixties'?
A   Women gaining the vote
B   Abortion law reform
C   Divorce law reform
D   Founding of the NHS

Question 11   Henry VII established the House of Tudor. What colour rose became the Tudor emblem?
A   Black
B   Red and white
C   Red
D   Yellow

Question 12   Which of the following statements is correct?
A   By the middle of the 17th century the last Welsh rebellions had been defeated
B   By the middle of the 15th century the last Welsh rebellions had been defeated

Question 13   Which of the following statements is correct?
A   The Battle of Agincourt is commemorated in the Bayeux Tapestry
B   The Battle of Hastings is commemorated in the Bayeux Tapestry

Question 14   Is the statement below TRUE or FALSE?
In 1833 a law abolished slavery throughout the British Empire

Question 15   D-Day refers to what event in British history?
A   Beginning of World War One
B   British invasion of Europe in 1944
C   Britain being invaded by the Romans
D   End of the war in Europe in 1945

Question 16   Which TWO developments were features of the Industrial Revolution?
A   Machinery
B   Increased farming
C   Changes in the law
D   Steam power

Question 17   After the abolition of slavery, more than 2 million migrants came from which TWO countries to replace the freed slaves?
A   Russia
B   India
C   China
D   Australia

Question 18   In which part of the British Empire did the Boer War of 1899–1902 take place?
A   India
B   Canada
C   Australia
D   South Africa

Question 19   Which of the following statements is correct?
A   By 1400 the preferred language of the English court was German
B   By 1400 the preferred language of the English court was English

Question 20   Which of the following statements is correct?
A   The Black Death was a plague that only had an impact in Ireland, where many people died
B   The Black Death brought about major changes in English society due to the number of people who died

British History
Practice Test 5

Question 1   Is the statement below TRUE or FALSE?
*Henry VIII is famous for marrying six times and breaking away from the
Church of Rome*

Question 2   In which battle during the First World War did the British suffer
60,000 casualties on the first day?
A   Agincourt
B   El Alamein
C   The Somme
D   Waterloo

Question 3   Which group of refugees settled in England before 1720?
A   Welsh
B   Germans
C   Jews
D   Huguenots

Question 4   Which TWO are 20th-century British discoveries or inventions?
A   Television
B   World Wide Web
C   Mobile phone
D   Petrol

Question 5   Which country did Germany invade in 1939 that led to the UK
declaring war on Germany?
A   Sweden
B   Finland
C   Poland
D   France

Question 6   Which of the following statements is correct?
A   James VI of Scotland was related to Queen Elizabeth I of England
B   James VI of Scotland was not related to Queen Elizabeth I of England

Question 7   Which TWO points about slavery are correct?
A   William Wilberforce was a leading abolitionist
B   Slavery survived in the British Empire until the early 21th century
C   Quakers set up the first anti-slavery groups
D   The Royal Navy refused to stop ships carrying slaves

Question 8   Is the statement below TRUE or FALSE?
   During the Great Depression of the 1930s the UK had high levels of
   employment

Question 9   Which colonies of the British Empire decided to declare their independence in 1776?
A   India
B   Canadian
C   American
D   South African

Question 10   Who invaded England in 1066?
A   Richard the Lionheart
B   Canute
C   William of Normandy
D   Harold of Wessex

Question 11   What happened to Margaret Thatcher in 1979 to make her famous in UK history?
A   She qualified as a barrister
B   She became a High Court judge
C   She became the first woman Prime Minister
D   She was made a general in the British army

Question 12   Which of the following statements is correct?
A   Henry VIII established the Church of England in order to start a war with the French
B   Henry VIII established the Church of England because the Pope refused to grant him a divorce

Question 13 Hadrian's Wall was built to keep out whom?
A The Irish
B The Welsh
C The Picts
D The Vikings

Question 14 The Enlightenment led to major developments in which TWO areas?
A Science
B Politics
C History
D English

Question 15 Which TWO groups contested the Wars of the Roses in the 15th century?
A Welsh
B House of York
C Scottish
D House of Lancaster

Question 16 What was the Beveridge Report of 1942 about?
A How to end the war in Europe
B How to re-unite Americans with their families after the war
C Establishing a Welfare State
D Overseas aid

Question 17 Is the statement below TRUE or FALSE?
  Catherine Howard was the sixth wife of Henry VIII

Question 18 What happened in 1215 to change the powers of the king?
A The Domesday Book
B Magna Carta
C The Reform Act
D The Black Death

Question 19 Who did Henry VIII marry after the execution of Anne Boleyn?
A Catherine Howard
B Catherine Parr
C Anne of Cleves
D Jane Seymour

Question 20   How old was Edward VI when he died?
A   15
B   18
C   21
D   35

Answers

Practice Test 1: British History

Question 1	A		Question 11	FALSE
Question 2	B and D		Question 12	TRUE
Question 3	B		Question 13	A
Question 4	B		Question 14	B
Question 5	C		Question 15	B and D
Question 6	B		Question 16	A
Question 7	B and C		Question 17	D
Question 8	FALSE		Question 18	B and C
Question 9	B		Question 19	TRUE
Question 10	A		Question 20	C

Practice Test 2: British History

Question 1	C and D		Question 11	FALSE
Question 2	A		Question 12	C
Question 3	B		Question 13	B
Question 4	A and D		Question 14	TRUE
Question 5	B		Question 15	A
Question 6	TRUE		Question 16	B and C
Question 7	A		Question 17	C
Question 8	B and C		Question 18	FALSE
Question 9	B		Question 19	C
Question 10	B		Question 20	A

Practice Test 3: British History

Question 1	FALSE		Question 11	B
Question 2	C		Question 12	TRUE
Question 3	FALSE		Question 13	TRUE
Question 4	A		Question 14	A and D
Question 5	A		Question 15	B
Question 6	FALSE		Question 16	B
Question 7	A and C		Question 17	TRUE
Question 8	B		Question 18	C and D
Question 9	B		Question 19	B
Question 10	A and B		Question 20	B

Practice Test 4: British History

Question 1	FALSE		Question 11	B
Question 2	TRUE		Question 12	B
Question 3	C and D		Question 13	B
Question 4	A		Question 14	TRUE
Question 5	TRUE		Question 15	B
Question 6	A		Question 16	A and D
Question 7	A		Question 17	B and C
Question 8	B and C		Question 18	D
Question 9	TRUE		Question 19	B
Question 10	B and C		Question 20	B

Practice Test 5: British History

Question 1	TRUE		Question 11	C
Question 2	C		Question 12	B
Question 3	D		Question 13	C
Question 4	A and B		Question 14	A and B
Question 5	C		Question 15	B and D
Question 6	A		Question 16	C
Question 7	A and C		Question 17	FALSE
Question 8	FALSE		Question 18	B
Question 9	C		Question 19	D
Question 10	C		Question 20	A

Section 2

British Politics and Principles

	page
Practice Test 1	25
Practice Test 2	29
Practice Test 3	32
Practice Test 4	35
Practice Test 5	38
Answers	42

British Politics and Principles
Practice Test 1

Question 1   Is the statement below TRUE or FALSE?
The British Constitution is contained in a single piece of legislation

Question 2   What happened in1999 to hereditary peers in the House of Lords?
A   Their numbers were greatly increased
B   Their salaries were stopped
C   Women were allowed to inherit their titles
D   They lost their automatic right to attend the House of Lords as peers

Question 3   Which TWO are political parties in the UK?
A   Logic Party
B   Campaign Party
C   Conservative Party
D   Labour Party

Question 4   How often does Prime Minister's Questions take place when Parliament is sitting?
A   Once a year
B   Twice a week
C   Once a week
D   Once a month

Question 5   What are TWO fundamental principles of British life?
A   Only riding your bike on weekdays
B   Participation in community life
C   Growing your own fruit and vegetables
D   Tolerance of those with different faiths and beliefs

Question 6   Which TWO are members of Parliament (MPs) responsible for?
A   Representing everyone in their constituency
B   Scrutinising and commenting on what the government is doing
C   Representing no one who voted for them
D   Supporting the government on all decisions and laws

Question 7   Which TWO of the following do pressure and lobby groups do?
A   Organise violent protests
B   Influence government policy
C   Assist the Prime Minister in his constituency work
D   Represent the views of British businesses

Question 8   Which of the following statements is correct?
A   Self-employed people need to pay National Insurance Contributions themselves
B   Self-employed people do not have to pay their National Insurance Contributions

Question 9   How are local councils funded?
A   Through money raised from charity events
B   Through donations from local people who are rich
C   From central government and local taxes
D   From local businesses only

Question 10   What type of government was formed after the General Election of 2010?
A   National Front party
B   All-party
C   Green party
D   Coalition

Question 11   What is the aim of the United Nations?
A   To create a single country
B   To prevent war and promote international peace and security
C   To examine decisions made by the European Union
D   To promote dictatorship

Question 12   Which of the following statements is correct?
A   The UK is governed by the parliament sitting at Westminster
B   The UK is governed by parliaments sitting in Scotland, Wales, and Northern Ireland

Question 13   Which of the following is a fundamental principle of British life?
A   Extremism
B   Fairness
C   Intolerance of other cultures
D   Inequality

Question 14   In 1999 which TWO new national Assemblies/Bodies were established?
A   Northern Ireland Assembly
B   Welsh Assembly
C   Scottish Parliament
D   American Assembly

Question 15   Which TWO chambers form the UK Parliament?
A   House of Fraser
B   House of Lords
C   House of Commons
D   House of Representatives

Question 16   Which TWO issues can the Welsh Assembly and the Scottish Parliament pass laws on?
A   Health
B   Education
C   Foreign Affairs
D   Immigration

Question 17   What TWO freedoms are offered by the UK to citizens and permanent residents?
A   Free holidays for up to two years
B   Freedom of speech
C   Free groceries for everyone
D   A right to a fair trial

Question 18   When is a by-election for a parliamentary seat held?
A   The Beginning of a parliamentary term
B   Every three years
C   When a member of Parliament (MP) dies or resigns
D   When the Prime Minister decides to call one

Question 19   What must you do in order to vote in elections?
A   Pay income tax for five years
B   Put your name on the electoral register
C   Register your identity with the police
D   Register yourself with the Home Office

Question 20   At what age can you vote in a General Election in the UK?
A   17
B   18
C   21
D   25

British Politics and Principles
Practice Test 2

Question 1 Which TWO services are funded by National Insurance Contributions?

A   Local taxi services
B   State retirement pension
C   Grocery delivery service
D   National Health Service (NHS)

Question 2   Is the following statement TRUE or FALSE?
   British values and principles are based on history and traditions

Question 3   Where is the National Assembly for Wales based?
A   Swansea
B   Newport
C   London
D   Cardiff

Question 4   Is the statement below TRUE or FALSE?
   The main political parties actively look for members to join their party

Question 5   How often are elections for the European Parliament held?
A   Annually
B   Every three years
C   Every five years
D   Every seven years

Question 6   How often are members of Parliament (MPs) elected?

A   At least every three years

B   Every six years

C   Every year

D   At least every five years

Question 7   Which TWO political parties formed the coalition government in 2010?

A   Conservatives

B   Labour

C   The National Front

D   Liberal Democrats

Question 8   Is the statement below TRUE or FALSE?

In the UK a citizen may only follow Roman Catholicism

Question 9   Is the statement below TRUE or FALSE?

A public vote in 2002 decided that Winston Churchill was the Greatest Briton of all time

Question 10   Which of the following statements is correct?

A   A free press means that what is written in newspapers is free from government control

B   A free press means newspapers are given out free of charge on Sundays

Question 11   Which of the following statements is correct?

A   The Speaker of the House of Commons remains a Member of Parliament (MP) after election as Speaker

B   The Speaker of the House of Commons has to give up being an MP when elected as Speaker

Question 12   How old do you need to be in order to stand for public office?

A   19

B   18

C   25

D   21

Question 13   Is the statement below TRUE or FALSE?

In the UK you are expected to respect the rights of others to have their own opinions

Question 14   Which of the following statements is correct?
A   The UK is a member of NATO
B   The UK has never been a member of NATO

Question 15   Who opens the new parliamentary session each year?
A   The Archbishop of Canterbury
B   The Prime Minister
C   The Speaker of the House of Commons
D   The Queen

Question 16   What TWO values are upheld by the Commonwealth association of countries?
A   Democracy
B   Dictatorship
C   Violent protest
D   Rule of law

Question 17   Is the statement below TRUE or FALSE?
Emmeline Pankhurst is famous for her leadership of the campaign to give women the vote in parliamentary elections in the UK

Question 18   Which of the following statements is correct?
A   Members of Parliament (MPs) are elected through a system called 'first past the post'
B   MPs are elected through a system called 'the winner takes it all'

Question 19   Which TWO principles are included in the European Convention on Human Rights?
A   Prohibition of slavery and forced labour
B   Freedom of thought, conscience and religion
C   The right to use violence if you think it is necessary
D   Freedom to leave work when you're going to a party

Question 20   Is the following statement TRUE or FALSE?
There is no place in British society for extremism or intolerance

British Politics and Principles
Practice Test 3

Question 1   Which of the following statements is correct?
A   The public can attend debates in the House of Commons
B   For a fee members of the public are allowed to attend debates in the House of Commons

Question 2   By joining a political party, what TWO activities might you be involved in?
A   Violent clashes with other political parties
B   Sitting next to your MP for sessions in the House of Commons
C   Handing out leaflets in the street
D   Knocking on people's doors and asking for support

Question 3   Which TWO of the following issues can the Northern Ireland Assembly make decisions on?
A   Defence
B   Environment
C   Foreign affairs
D   Social services

Question 4   What system of government does the UK have?
A   Communist government
B   Dictatorship
C   Parliamentary democracy
D   Federal government

Question 5   When a Member of Parliament (MP) dies or resigns, what is the election called that is held to replace them?
A   Re-selection
B   Re-election
C   Fresh Start
D   By-election

Question 6   Which of the following statements is correct?
A   Civil Servants are politically neutral
B   Civil servants must obey whatever orders the Prime Minister gives

Question 7   Is the statement below TRUE or FALSE?
   Being kind and helpful to your neighbours can help you gain respect within the community

Question 8   Which of the following statements is correct?
A   The UK offers its citizens and permanent residents freedom of speech
B   The UK does not allow citizens or permanent residents to voice opinions for the first five years

Question 9   Is the statement below TRUE or FALSE?
   Participating in your community is a fundamental principle of British life

Question 10   Who were the 'suffragettes'?
A   Women who left the UK to live in India
B   Women who campaigned for women's votes
C   Women who chose to be single
D   Women who stayed at home as housewives

Question 11   Which TWO changes were introduced by the Education Act of 1944?
A   New examination fees
B   Primary education for under 16 year olds
C   Free secondary education for all
D   A clear division between primary and secondary education

Question 12   Which of the following statements is correct?
A   Members of the House of Lords are elected by the public
B   Members of the House of Lords are voted in by members of the House of Commons

Question 13 Is the statement below TRUE or FALSE?

Wales and Scotland each have developed administrations which give them total control over all policies and laws

Question 14 Which of the following statements is correct?
A The official home of the Prime Minister is 10 Downing Street
B The official home of the Prime Minister is 11 Downing Street

Question 15 Which TWO of the following groups of adults are eligible to vote in all UK elections?
A UK-born and settled adult citizens
B Only those born in the UK
C Citizens of the Commonwealth who are residents in the UK
D Visitors to the UK

Question 16 Who currently appoints life peers in the House of Lords?
A The Queen
B The Prime Minister
C The Speaker of the House of Commons
D Members of Parliament (MPs)

Question 17 To which TWO international bodies does the UK belong?
A The North Atlantic Treaty Organization (NATO)
B The Commonwealth
C The North American Free Trade Agreement (NAFTA)
D The Indian League

Question 18 Is the statement below TRUE or FALSE?

You can support your local community by becoming a school governor or school board member

Question 19 Which of the following statements is correct?
A The Queen is a ceremonial head of the Commonwealth
B The Queen is the head of the European Union

Question 20 Is the statement below TRUE or FALSE?

British has never been at war with France

British Politics and Principles
Practice Test 4

Question 1 Which of the following statements is correct?

A   In 1998 the Good Friday Agreement devolved powers to Scotland

B   In 1998 the Good Friday Agreement led to the establishment of the Northern Ireland Assembly

Question 2 Which area of government policy is the responsibility of the Chancellor of the Exchequer?

A   Education

B   Health

C   Economy

D   Foreign affairs

Question 3 Is the statement below TRUE or FALSE?

Members of the armed forces cannot stand for public office

Question 4 Which TWO of the following are part of the UK government?

A   The cabinet

B   The civil service

C   NATO

D   FIFA

Question 5 What happens when members of Parliament (MPs) hold surgeries?

A   They meet local doctors discuss local health issues
B   Members of the public can meet their MP to discuss issues
C   They discuss new medical procedures with surgeons
D   They invite members of the press along to talk over national issues

Question 6   Is the statement below TRUE or FALSE?
If you are a Commonwealth citizen living in the UK you can vote in all public elections

Question 7   The term 'suffragettes' is associated with which group of people?
A   Men
B   Women
C   Children
D   Migrants

Question 8   Which of the following statements is correct?
A   There are a few members of Parliament who do not represent any of the main political parties
B   All members of Parliament have to belong to a political party

Question 9   Is the statement below TRUE or FALSE?
The Home Secretary is the government minister responsible for managing relationships with foreign countries

Question 10   Which of the following statements is correct?
A   Proceedings in Parliament cannot be reported in the press
B   Proceedings in Parliament are broadcast on television

Question 11   Which of the following statements is correct?
A   Decisions on government policies are made by the Queen
B   Decisions on government policies are made by the Prime Minister and cabinet and then approved by the Queen

Question 12   Is the statement below TRUE or FALSE?
Pressure and lobby groups try to influence British government policy

Question 13   Which of the following statements is correct?
A   The civil service largely consists of political appointees
B   The civil service is politically neutral

Question 14   How is the Speaker of the House of Commons chosen?
A   By the Queen
B   By the police
C   In a secret ballot
D   By the Prime Minister

Question 15   Is the statement below TRUE or FALSE?
Margaret Thatcher was the longest-serving UK Prime Minister of the 20th century known as the Iron Lady

Question 16   Which of the following statements is correct?
A   It is free to visit the Houses of Parliament to watch debates
B   It costs £25 to visit the Houses of Parliament to watch debates

Question 17   Which TWO responsibilities should you respect as a resident of the UK?
A   Respect and obey the law
B   Treat others with fairness
C   Carry out violent protest
D   Take in and look after sick people

Question 18   Which of the following statements is correct?
A   The Chancellor of the Exchequer is responsible for crime, policing and immigration
B   The Chancellor of the Exchequer is responsible for the economy

Question 19   What happens when a Member of Parliament (MP) dies or resigns?
A   The post remains vacant until the next General Election
B   Their party chooses anybody to fill the post until the next General Election
C   A by-election is held to replace the MP
D   A neighbouring MP looks after the constituency

Question 20   Is the statement below TRUE or FALSE?
The House of Lords must act as the government wishes

British Politics and Principles
Practice Test 5

Question 1   Is the statement below TRUE or FALSE?
A General Election occurs every ten years

Question 2   Which of the following statements is correct?
A   In Wales a member of your family must complete a voting registration form on your behalf
B   In Wales all those entitled to vote must complete their own registration form

Question 3   Which of the following statements is correct?
A   All Acts of Parliament are made in the monarch's name
B   All Acts of Parliament are made in the Prime Minister's name

Question 4   Which parts of the United Kingdom have devolved governments?
A   Only Wales
B   Wales, England and Northern Ireland
C   Only Northern Ireland
D   Wales, Scotland and Northern Ireland

Question 5   What age group does the National Citizen Service programme cover?
A   All children up to the age of 18
B   Pensioners
C   16- and 17- year olds
D   21 year olds

Question 6   What is a fundamental principle of British life?
A   A relaxed work ethic every Friday
B   Democracy
C   Extremism
D   Religious faith

Question 7   Is the statement below TRUE or FALSE?
The developed Scottish government rules Scotland from Edinburgh

Question 8   Which of the following statements is correct?
A   Local elections are normally held in May
B   Local elections are normally held at Christmas

Question 9   Is the statement below TRUE or FALSE?
Life peers in the House of Lords can pass their title to their children after 1999

Question 10   Which of the following countries did not help to set up the EEC?
A   Ireland
B   Luxemburg
C   Belgium
D   Germany

Question 11   How are local authorities funded?
A   By funding from central government only
B   By charities only
C   By central government funding and by taxation
D   Local authorities are unfunded

Question 12   Who chairs debates in the House of Commons?
A   The leader of the opposition
B   The Prime Minister
C   The Speaker
D   The Foreign Secretary

Question 13   MPs have a duty to serve and represent which of the following people?
A   Their fellow MPs
B   Everyone in their constituency
C   Everyone in their constituency who voted for them
D   Everyone who helped them

Question 14   Is the statement below TRUE or FALSE?
   The Bill of Rights confirmed the rights of Parliament and the limits of the king's power

Question 15   Which of the following is one of the Queen's important ceremonial roles?
A   To chair debates in Parliament
B   To sit in European Parliament
C   To receive foreign ambassadors and high commissioners
D   To negotiate trade agreements with other countries

Question 16   Is the statement below TRUE or FALSE?
   'The Council of Europe has the power to make laws, which are binding in member states'

Question 17   After the Act of Union, Scotland was no longer an independent country. In what TWO ways was it still separate from the rest of Great Britain?
A   It kept its own army
B   It kept its own educational system
C   It kept its Presbyterian Church
D   Hadrian's Wall was rebuilt to secure the border

Question 18   Is the statement below TRUE or FALSE?
   The candidate who wins the most votes is elected MP for the constituency

Question 19   How many people make up a Scottish jury?
A   10
B   12
C   15
D   18

Question 20   The Welsh Assembly and the Scottish Parliament make decisions in which TWO of the following areas?

A   Agriculture

B   Nuclear Energy

C   Foreign Policy

D   The environment

Answers

Practice Test 1: British Politics and Principles

Question 1	FALSE	Question 11	B
Question 2	D	Question 12	A
Question 3	C and D	Question 13	B
Question 4	C	Question 14	B and C
Question 5	B and D	Question 15	B and C
Question 6	A and B	Question 16	A and B
Question 7	B and D	Question 17	B and D
Question 8	A	Question 18	C
Question 9	C	Question 19	B
Question 10	D	Question 20	B

Practice Test 2: British Politics and Principles

Question 1	B and D	Question 11	A
Question 2	TRUE	Question 12	B
Question 3	D	Question 13	TRUE
Question 4	TRUE	Question 14	A
Question 5	C	Question 15	D
Question 6	D	Question 16	A and D
Question 7	A and D	Question 17	TRUE
Question 8	FALSE	Question 18	A
Question 9	TRUE	Question 19	A and B
Question 10	A	Question 20	TRUE

Practice Test 3: British Politics and Principles

Question 1	A		Question 11	C and D
Question 2	C and D		Question 12	A
Question 3	B and D		Question 13	FALSE
Question 4	C		Question 14	A
Question 5	D		Question 15	A and C
Question 6	A		Question 16	A
Question 7	TRUE		Question 17	A and B
Question 8	A		Question 18	TRUE
Question 9	TRUE		Question 19	A
Question 10	B		Question 20	FALSE

Practice Test 4: British Politics and Principles

Question 1	B		Question 11	B
Question 2	C		Question 12	TRUE
Question 3	TRUE		Question 13	B
Question 4	A and B		Question 14	C
Question 5	B		Question 15	TRUE
Question 6	TRUE		Question 16	A
Question 7	B		Question 17	A and B
Question 8	A		Question 18	B
Question 9	FALSE		Question 19	C
Question 10	B		Question 20	FALSE

Practice Test 5: British Politics and Principles

Question 1	FALSE		Question 11	C
Question 2	B		Question 12	C
Question 3	A		Question 13	B
Question 4	D		Question 14	TRUE
Question 5	C		Question 15	C
Question 6	B		Question 16	FALSE
Question 7	TRUE		Question 17	B and C
Question 8	A		Question 18	TRUE
Question 9	FALSE		Question 19	C
Question 10	A		Question 20	A and D

Section 3

British Culture and Entertainment

	page
Practice Test 1	47
Practice Test 2	50
Practice Test 3	53
Practice Test 4	57
Answers	60

British Culture and Entertainment
Practice Test 1

Question 1 Which of the following statements is correct?

A *Eastenders* and *Coronation Street* are popular television programmes known as 'soaps'

B *Eastenders* and *Coronation Street* are historical landmarks

Question 2 For which TWO types of literature is William Shakespeare famous?

A Novels

B Plays

C Biographies

D Sonnets

Question 3 Is the statement below TRUE or FALSE?

British scientists were the first to clone a mammal successfully. The animal was a rabbit.

Question 4 Which stories are associated with Geoffrey Chaucer?

A *The Scottish Tales*

B *The Oxford Tales*

C *The London Tales*

D *The Canterbury Tales*

Question 5 Which of the following statements is correct?

A Both Jane Austen and Charles Dickens are famous novelists

B Both Jane Austen and Charles Dickens are famous landscape artists

Question 6   Is the statement below TRUE or FALSE?

The Brit Awards are annual pop music awards

Question 7   Which of the following statements is correct?

A   Gilbert and Sullivan were famous British sailors

B   Gilbert and Sullivan wrote many comic operas

Question 8   Is the statement below TRUE or FALSE?

The Union Flag comprises four crosses, one for each part of the United Kingdom

Question 9   Is the statement below TRUE or FALSE?

Some people rent land called 'an allotment', where they grow fruit and vegetables

Question 10   Which of the following statements is correct?

A   There is a yearly swimming race on the River Thames between Oxford and Cambridge Universities

B   There is a yearly rowing race on the River Thames between Oxford and Cambridge Universities

Question 11   Which TWO are plays by William Shakespeare?

A   *Hamlet*

B   *Bleak House*

C   *Romeo and Juliet*

D   *Oliver Twist*

Question 12   Which of the following statements is correct?

A   Volunteering is a good way to earn additional money

B   Volunteering is a way of helping others without receiving payment

Question 13   Which is the most popular sport in the UK?

A   Football

B   Horse Racing

C   Golf

D   Tennis

Question 14   Which of the following statements is correct?

A   The Proms is an eight-week summer season of orchestral music

B   The Proms are a series of tennis matches held every June in London

Question 15   Which TWO of the following are famous British authors?
A   Sir Steve Redgrave
B   Gustav Holst
C   Sir Arthur Conan Doyle
D   J K Rowling

Question 16   Which TWO of the following are linked to football?
A   The British Grand Prix
B   UEFA
C   Premier League
D   Royal Ascot

Question 17   What is the name of a novel by Jane Austen?
A   *Sense and Sensibility*
B   *Far from the Madding Crowd*
C   *Oliver Twist*
D   *Romeo and Juliet*

Question 18   Which of the following statements is correct?
A   Lancelot 'Capability' Brown and Gertrude Jekyll were famous garden designers
B   Lancelot 'Capability' Brown and Gertrude Jekyll were famous characters in a Sherlock Holmes story

Question 19   What are *Beowulf, The Tyger* and *She Walks in Beauty*?
A   Plays
B   Films
C   Poems
D   Musicals

Question 20   Which of the following statements is correct?
A   *The Mousetrap* is a play that has been running in London's West End since 1952
B   *The Mousetrap* is a countryside policy aimed at trapping mice for animal testing

British Culture and Entertainment
Practice Test 2

Question 1 Is the statement below TRUE or FALSE?
Isaac Newton is a famous singer from the 18th century

Question 2 Which TWO of the following are major horse-racing events in the UK?
A   The Open Championship
B   Scottish Grand National
C   Six Nations Championship
D   Royal Ascot

Question 3 What awards event celebrates British theatre?
A   The Laurence Olivier Awards
B   The Turner Prize
C   The Brit Awards
D   The Man Booker Prize

Question 4 Which TWO people are famous UK sports stars?
A   Sir Chris Hoy
B   Dame Kelly Holmes
C   Anthony Hopkins
D   Jane Austen

Question 5 Which TWO of the following are major outdoor music festivals?
A   Royal Ascot
B   Isle of Wight Festival
C   Hogmanay
D   Glastonbury

Question 6   Which of the following statements is correct?

A   Sake Dean Mahomet is famous for introducing pubs and cinemas to Britain from India

B   Sake Dean Mahomet introduced curry houses and shampooing to Britain from India

Question 7   What do Sir William Golding, Seamus Heaney and Harold Pinter have in common?

A   They are all famous British gymnasts

B   They have all been Prime Minister

C   They were part of the first British expedition to the South Pole

D   They have all been awarded the Nobel Prize for literature

Question 8   Which TWO of the following were British inventions?

A   Television

B   Jet engine

C   Personal computer

D   Diesel engine

Question 9   Is the statement below TRUE or FALSE?

Mo Farah and Jessica Ennis are well known athletes who won gold medals at the 2012 London Olympics

Question 10   Which of the following statements is correct?

A   Sir Steve Redgrave is a famous rower who won gold medals in five consecutive Olympic Games

B   Sir Steve Redgrave is a famous British Scientist who discovered penicillin

Question 11   Which TWO are 20th-century British discoveries or inventions?

A   Hovercraft

B   Rockets

C   Penicillin

D   Printing press

Question 12   Which of the following statements is correct?

A   Andy Murray is the first British man to walk around the world

B   Andy Murray is the first British man to win a singles tennis title in a Grand Slam tournament since 1936

Question 13 Is the statement below TRUE or FALSE?
Thomas Hardy is a famous author who wrote Tess of the d'Urbervilles

Question 14 Which of the following statements is correct?
A   George and Robert Stephenson were famous pioneers of railway engines
B   George and Robert Stephenson were famous pioneers of aviation

Question 15 Which TWO things can you do to look after your environment?
A   Drive your car as much as possible
B   Recycle your waste
C   Never turn the lights off in your house
D   Walk, cycle and use public transport to get around

Question 16 What was Isambard Kingdom Brunel famous for designing and building?
A   Motor bikes
B   Helicopters
C   Bridges
D   Skyscrapers

Question 17 Is the statement below TRUE or FALSE?
Charles Dickens is famous for writing musicals

Question 18 Which of the following statements is correct?
A   Rugby was introduced to ancient Britain by Roman invaders
B   Rugby originated in England in the early 19th century

Question 19 Is the statement below TRUE or FALSE?
William Blake, Lord Byron and Robert Browning were all famous rowers

Question 20 Which of the following statements is correct?
A   Cricket matches can last up to five days
B   Cricket matches can last up to ten weeks

British Culture and Entertainment
Practice Test 3

Question 1   Which jubilee did Queen Elizabeth II celebrate in 2012?
A   Ruby Jubilee
B   Diamond Jubilee
C   Silver Jubilee
D   Golden Jubilee

Question 2   Which is the UK's most popular sport?
A   Boxing
B   Golf
C   Rugby
D   Football

Question 3   What are the titles of TWO novels by Charles Dickens?
A   *Harry Potter*
B   *Lord of the Rings*
C   *A Christmas Carol*
D   *Oliver Twist*

Question 4   How can you reduce your carbon footprint?
A   Shop locally for products
B   Buy duty-free products when you're abroad
C   Do all your shopping online
D   Drive to the supermarket

Question 5   What are the TWO benefits of volunteering?
A   Earning additional money
B   Meeting new people
C   You are given lots of gifts
D   Making your community a better place

Question 6   Which TWO of the following are famous British artists?
A   Andy Murray
B   David Hockney
C   Sir Edward Elgar
D   Henry Moore

Question 7   Is the statement below TRUE or FALSE?
   The British Broadcasting Corporation (BBC) is financed by selling advertising space during television programmes

Question 8   Bobby Moore is famous for his achievements in which sport?
A   Football
B   Rugby union
C   Golf
D   Cricket

Question 9   Which TWO are famous British fashion designers?
A   Mary Quant
B   Winston Churchill
C   Jane Austen
D   Vivienne Westwood

Question 10   In everyday language people may say, 'rain stopped play'. Which sport is this phrase associated?
A   Football
B   Cricket
C   Rugby league
D   Sailing

Question 11   Is the statement below TRUE or FALSE?
   Shakespeare was a great English playwright

Question 12   Which TWO of the following were important 20th-century inventors?

A   Alan Turing
B   Tim Berners-Lee
C   George Stephenson
D   Isambard Kingdom Brunel

Question 13   Which sport can be traced back to 15th-century Scotland?

A   Surfing
B   Formula 1
C   Golf
D   Motorbike racing

Question 14   Which of the following statements is correct?

A   Several British writers have won the Nobel Prize in Literature
B   No British writer has won the Nobel Prize in Literature

Question 15   What is one of the roles of school governors and school boards?

A   Setting the strategic direction of the school
B   Driving the school bus
C   Giving teachers ideas for lesson plans
D   Serving food and drink in the canteen

Question 16   What are the names of TWO famous British film actors?

A   Daniel Day Lewis
B   Paula Radcliffe
C   Colin Firth
D   Robert Louis Stevenson

Question 17   In which modern-day country was the composer George Frederick Handel born?

A   Iceland
B   Russia
C   Japan
D   Germany

Question 18   Since 1927 the BBC has organised which series of famous concerts?

A   The Eisteddfod
B   Aldeburgh Festival
C   The Proms
D   Glastonbury

Question 19   Which TWO are famous horse-racing events?

A   The Grand National
B   The FA Cup
C   Royal Ascot
D   The Six Nations

Question 20   Who are TWO famous British film directors?

A   Sir Alfred Hitchcock
B   Gordon Brown
C   Ridley Scott
D   Isambard Kingdom Brunel

British Culture and Entertainment
Practice Test 4

Question 1 Which TWO of the following are famous Paralympians?
A Steve Redgrave
B Ellie Simmonds
C Baroness Tanni Grey-Thompson
D Dame Ellen MacArthur

Question 2 Which of the following statements is correct?
A The BBC is funded through advertisements and subscriptions
B The BBC is the only wholly state-funded media organisation

Question 3 Dylan Thomas was a famous writer and poet from which country?
A England
B Scotland
C Wales
D Northern Ireland

Question 4 Is the statement below TRUE or FALSE?
The Wimbledon Championships are associated with tennis

Question 5 Which TWO were great thinkers of the Enlightenment?
A Robert Burns
B Robert Louis Stevenson
C Adam Smith
D David Hume

Question 6   With which sport do you associate Lewis Hamilton, Jensen Button and Damon Hill?
A   Rugby
B   Athletics
C   Skiing
D   Formula 1

Question 7   Which TWO are famous British authors?
A   Charles Dickens
B   Graham Greene
C   Mary Quant
D   Henry Moore

Question 8   Which TWO genres is William Shakespeare famous for writing?
A   Plays
B   TV dramas
C   Poems
D   Radio scripts

Question 9   Which TWO are influential British bands?
A   Elton John
B   The Rolling Stones
C   The Beatles
D   The Conservatives

Question 10   What is a traditional pub game in the UK?
A   Scrabble
B   Pool
C   Table tennis
D   Polo

Question 11   Is the statement below TRUE or FALSE?
   Boys in the UK leave school with better qualifications than girls

Question 12   Which of the following statements is correct?
A   Shakespeare wrote 'To be or not to be'
B   Shakespeare wrote 'We will fight them on the beaches'

Question 13   Why is Sir Edwin Lutyens famous?
A   He was the first man to land on the moon
B   He was the first UK Prime Minister
C   He invented the World Wide Web
D   He was a 20th-century architect

Question 14   Which of the following statements is correct?
A   Women in the UK make up about an eighth of the workforce
B   Women in Britain make up about half of the workforce

Question 15   Which UK city hosted the 2012 Paralympic games?
A   Manchester
B   Swansea
C   Edinburgh
D   London

Question 16   Is the statement below TRUE or FALSE?
Britain and Germany developed Concorde, a passenger supersonic aircraft

Question 17   Which TWO are famous British composers?
A   Wolfgang Amadeus Mozart
B   Frederic Chopin
C   Henry Purcell
D   Ralph Vaughan Williams

Question 18   Which of these people was a great British playwright?
A   Sir Francis Drake
B   Geoffrey Chaucer
C   William Caxton
D   William Shakespere

Question 19   Which of these statements is correct?
A   Refuges and shelters offer a safe place to stay for victims of domestic violence
B   The Citizens Advice Bureau offers a safe place to stay for victims of domestic violence

Question 20   When were the first professional football clubs formed?
A   16th century
B   15th century
C   19th century
D   20th century

Answers

Practice Test 1: British Culture and Entertainment

Question 1	A		Question 11	A and C
Question 2	B and D		Question 12	B
Question 3	FALSE		Question 13	A
Question 4	D		Question 14	A
Question 5	A		Question 15	C and D
Question 6	TRUE		Question 16	B and C
Question 7	B		Question 17	A
Question 8	FALSE		Question 18	A
Question 9	TRUE		Question 19	C
Question 10	B		Question 20	A

Practice Test 2: British Culture and Entertainment

Question 1	FALSE		Question 11	A and C
Question 2	B and D		Question 12	B
Question 3	A		Question 13	TRUE
Question 4	A and B		Question 14	A
Question 5	B and D		Question 15	B and D
Question 6	B		Question 16	C
Question 7	D		Question 17	FALSE
Question 8	A and B		Question 18	B
Question 9	TRUE		Question 19	FALSE
Question 10	A		Question 20	A

Practice Test 3: British Culture and Entertainment

Question 1	B		Question 11	TRUE
Question 2	D		Question 12	A and B
Question 3	C and D		Question 13	C
Question 4	A		Question 14	A
Question 5	B and D		Question 15	A
Question 6	B and D		Question 16	A and C
Question 7	FALSE		Question 17	D
Question 8	A		Question 18	C
Question 9	A and D		Question 19	A and C
Question 10	B		Question 20	A and C

Practice Test 4: British Culture and Entertainment

Question 1	B and C		Question 11	FALSE
Question 2	B		Question 12	A
Question 3	C		Question 13	D
Question 4	TRUE		Question 14	B
Question 5	C and D		Question 15	D
Question 6	D		Question 16	FALSE
Question 7	A and B		Question 17	C and D
Question 8	A and C		Question 18	D
Question 9	B and C		Question 19	A
Question 10	B		Question 20	C

Section 4
British Law

	page
Practice Test 1	65
Practice Test 2	68
Practice Test 3	72
Answers	75

British Law
Practice Test 1

Question 1 Is the statement below TRUE or FALSE?
In the UK betting and gambling are legal

Question 2 What sorts of cases do Crown Courts and Sheriff Courts deal with?
A Small claims procedures
B Youth cases
C Divorce hearings
D Serious offences

Question 3 What is the minimum age for jury service?
A 17
B 18
C 16
D 25

Question 4 Is the statement below TRUE or FALSE?
An example of a civil law case is when you have purchased a faulty item and made a legal complaint

Question 5 Which of the following statements is correct?
A Police and Crime Commissioners (PCCs) are appointed through a public election
B Police and Crime Commissioners (PCCs) are appointed by the Monarch

Question 6 Which of the following statements is correct?
A You have to be aged 17 or over to buy a National Lottery ticket
B You have to be aged 16 or over to buy a National Lottery ticket

Question 7 Which of the following do you need in order to gain a full car licence?

A   Pass a driving test which tests both knowledge and practical skills
B   Own a car
C   Achieve five GCSE passes
D   Have a Degree

Question 8 Which of the following areas does civil law cover?

A   Debt
B   Violent crime
C   Armed Robbery
D   Murder

Question 9 What is the minimum legal age you can buy alcohol in the UK?

A   17
B   21
C   18
D   16

Question 10 What is a responsibility that you will have as a citizen or permanent resident of the UK?

A   To attend a Church
B   To avoid shopping on a Sunday
C   To look after yourself and your family
D   To grow your own fruit and vegetables

Question 11 Which of the following statements is correct?

A   In a Crown Court case the judge decides the sentence when someone is guilty
B   In a Crown Court case the jury decides the sentence if someone is found guilty

Question 12 Is the statement below TRUE or FALSE?
   Discrimination in the workplace is an example of criminal law

Question 13 Which of these statements is correct?

A   Only Self-Employed people pay National Insurance Contributions
B   Most working people pay National Insurance Contributions

Question 14   Which of the following provide legal advice, normally for a fee?
A   Prison Guards
B   Magistrates
C   Solicitors
D   Community Police Officers

Question 15   The judiciary is responsible for which TWO of the following?
A   Interpreting the law
B   Making the law
C   Managing prisons
D   Making sure that trials are fair

Question 16   In a Crown Court, who decides what the penalty will be, in the case of a 'guilty' verdict?
A   The court usher
B   The judge
C   The jury
D   A police officer

Question 17   Is a verdict of 'not proven' possible?
A   Yes, but only in a Magistrates' Court
B   Yes, but only in Scotland

Question 18   Is it acceptable in the UK to treat people worse because of their sexual orientation?
A   Yes, if their sexual orientation is forbidden by religion
B   No, it is never acceptable to treat people worse for their sexual orientation

Question 19   Is the statement below TRUE or FALSE?
You have to be 17 or over to buy a drink in a public house (pub) or nightclub

Question 20   Is the statement below TRUE or FALSE?
People over the age of 75 do not have to pay for a television licence

British Law
Practice Test 2

Question 1   Who has to pay National Insurance Contributions?
A   Everyone in the UK who is in paid work
B   People who work full-time
C   All those aged 50 and below
D   Pensioners who no longer work

Question 2   How old must you be to ride a moped in the UK?
A   17
B   21
C   16
D   22

Question 3   Which of the following statements is correct?
A   After the age of 70, drivers must renew their licence every three years
B   After the age of 70, drivers must renew their licence every six years

Question 4   If your car is more than three years old, how often will it need a Ministry of Transport (MOT) test?
A   Every four years
B   Every six months
C   Every ten years
D   Every year

Question 5   Is the statement below TRUE or FALSE?
   All young people are sent a National Insurance number just before their 16th birthday

Question 6   What is a jury made up of?
A   People who are very wealthy
B   People randomly chosen from the electoral register
C   People who own property
D   People who have submitted an application form and have passed an interview

Question 7   Which TWO of the following would you contact for legal advice?
A   A solicitor
B   A local councillor
C   The Citizens Advice Bureau
D   The National Trust

Question 8   In Scotland, how many people serve on a jury?
A   12
B   11
C   15
D   21

Question 9   Which of the following statements is correct?
A   On becoming a UK citizen or permanent resident, you can choose which laws and responsibilities you want to accept
B   On becoming a UK citizen or permanent resident, you will be agreeing to respect the laws, values and traditions in the UK

Question 10   Is the statement below TRUE or FALSE?
You can serve on a jury up to the age of 90

Question 11   Once you are aged 17 or older, which TWO vehicles can you learn to drive?
A   Motor cycle
B   Car
C   Fire engine
D   Heavy goods vehicle

Question 12   To apply for UK citizenship or permanent residency, which TWO things do you need?
A   A UK driving licence
B   An ability to speak and read English
C   A good understanding of life in the UK
D   A Degree in English

Question 13 Is the statement below TRUE or FALSE?
The legal systems in England, Wales, Scotland and Northern Ireland are exactly the same

Question 14 Which of the following statements is correct?
A   An example of a criminal offence is carrying a weapon
B   An example of a criminal offence is not paying your rent

Question 15 Which court would you use to get money back that was owed to you?
A   County Court
B   Magistrates' Court
C   Youth Court
D   Coroner's Court

Question 16 What TWO actions can a judge take if a public body is not respecting someone's legal rights?
A   Place its members in prison
B   Order them to change their practices
C   Order them to pay compensation
D   Close down the public body

Question 17 Which TWO courts deal with minor criminal cases in the UK?
A   Justice of the Peace Court
B   Family Court
C   Crown Court
D   Magistrates' Court

Question 18 What is a fundamental principle of British life?
A   The rule of law
B   The rule of the wealthy
C   The rule of the monarch
D   The rule of your local member of Parliament (MP)

Question 19 What must police officers do?
A   Be rude and abusive
B   Obey the law
C   Bribe witnesses
D   Use torture methods to obtain statements

Question 20   Who elects Police and Crime Commissioners (PCCs)?

A   The Monarch
B   The Home Office
C   The public
D   The police

British Law
Practice Test 3

Question 1 Which of the following statements is correct?
A The small claims procedure is an informal way of helping people to settle minor disputes
B The small claims procedure helps people to make small home insurance claims

Question 2 Is the statement below TRUE or FALSE?
  Members of the public are allowed to attend Youth Court hearings

Question 3 Which TWO are examples of civil law?
A Disputes between landlords and tenants
B Arson
C Discrimination in the workplace
D Grievous bodily harm

Question 4 Is the statement below TRUE or FALSE?
  The Scottish Parliament can pass legislation for Scotland on all matters

Question 5 Is the statement below TRUE or FALSE?
  People are able to buy National Lottery tickets in the UK if they are aged 15 or over

Question 6 Which TWO types of case are held in County Courts?
A Divorce
B Murder
C Minor criminal offences
D Breaches of contract

Question 7 Which of the following statements is correct?
A   UK laws ensure people are not treated unfairly in any area of work or life
B   In the UK, employers can discriminate against different groups of people

Question 8 Which TWO of the following do you have to pay tax on?
A   Profits from self-employment
B   Income from property, savings and dividends
C   Shopping vouchers given to you by family or friends
D   Small amounts of money given to you as a gift

Question 9 Which of the following statements is correct?
A   If your driving licence is from a country in the European Union you can drive in the UK for as long as the licence is valid
B   If your driving licence is from a country in the European Union you have to apply for a UK licence in order to drive

Question 10 Which of the following statements is correct?
A   Magistrates usually work unpaid and do not need legal qualifications
B   Magistrates must be qualified solicitors who have under gone further specialist magistrate training

Question 11 Which TWO of the following are examples of criminal law?
A   Racial Crime
B   Disputes about faulty goods
C   Selling tobacco to anyone under the age of 18
D   Gender discrimination in the workplace

Question 12 What is the minimum age you can drive a car or motor cycle in the UK?
A   17
B   21
C   18
D   26

Question 13 Is the statement below TRUE or FALSE?
   A husband who forces his wife to have sex can be charged with rape

Question 14 Which of the following statements is correct?
A   County Courts deal with criminal cases
B   County Courts deal with civil disputes

Question 15   Is the statement below TRUE or FALSE?
If a person is aged under 21, their case will be heard in a Youth Court

Question 16   When walking your dog in a public place, what must you ensure?
A   That your dog wears a blue dog coat
B   That your dog never strays more than 6 metres away from you
C   That your dog does not come into contact with other people
D   That your dog wears a collar showing the name and address of the owner

Question 17   What is the role of a jury at a Court trial?
A   To decide whether evidence should be allowed to be heard
B   To decide the sentence that the accused should be given
C   To decide who the judge should be
D   To decide whether the accused is 'guilty' or 'not guilty'

Question 18   Which TWO of the following are protected by law from discrimination?
A   Disability
B   Eye colour
C   Hair colour
D   Marital status

Question 19   Is the statement below TRUE or FALSE?
Forcing another person to marry is a criminal offence in the UK

Question 20   As well as giving legal advice, solicitors are able to do which TWO of the following?
A   Represent clients in court
B   Arrest suspects
C   Take action for a client
D   Decide sentence at Court

Answers

Practice Test 1: British Law

Question 1	TRUE		Question 11	A
Question 2	D		Question 12	FALSE
Question 3	B		Question 13	B
Question 4	TRUE		Question 14	C
Question 5	A		Question 15	A and D
Question 6	B		Question 16	B
Question 7	A		Question 17	B
Question 8	A		Question 18	B
Question 9	C		Question 19	FALSE
Question 10	C		Question 20	TRUE

Practice Test 2: British Law

Question 1	A		Question 11	A and B
Question 2	C		Question 12	B and C
Question 3	A		Question 13	FALSE
Question 4	D		Question 14	A
Question 5	TRUE		Question 15	A
Question 6	B		Question 16	B and C
Question 7	A and C		Question 17	A and D
Question 8	C		Question 18	A
Question 9	B		Question 19	B
Question 10	FALSE		Question 20	C

Practice Test 3: British Law

Question 1	A		Question 11	A and C
Question 2	FALSE		Question 12	A
Question 3	A and C		Question 13	TRUE
Question 4	FALSE		Question 14	B
Question 5	FALSE		Question 15	FALSE
Question 6	A and D		Question 16	D
Question 7	A		Question 17	D
Question 8	A and B		Question 18	A and D
Question 9	A		Question 19	TRUE
Question 10	A		Question 20	A and C

Section 5

British Geography and National Information

	page
Practice Test 1	79
Practice Test 2	82
Answers	86

British Geography and National Information
Practice Test 1

Question 1   Which TWO are famous UK landmarks?
A   Snowdonia
B   Eiffel Tower
C   Loch Lomond
D   Empire State Building

Question 2   Is the statement below TRUE or FALSE?
   Most People in the UK live in towns and cities

Question 3   Which TWO are British overseas territories?
A   Cyprus
B   Falkland Islands
C   St Helena
D   Italy

Question 4   Which of the following is a famous Stone Age site in the UK?
A   The Globe Theatre
B   Nelson's Column
C   Stonehenge
D   Windsor Castle

Question 5   St David is the patron saint of which country of the UK?
A   England
B   Scotland
C   Wales
D   Northern Ireland

Question 6   Is the statement below TRUE or FALSE?

There are many variations in language in the different parts of the UK

Question 7   Which of the following is a country of the UK?

A   Channel Islands
B   Scotland
C   Isle of Man
D   Republic of Ireland

Question 8   Is the statement below TRUE or FALSE?

Northern Ireland and Scotland have their own banknotes

Question 9   Is the statement below TRUE or FALSE?

Snowdonia is a national park in Scotland

Question 10   Which TWO countries are members of the Commonwealth?

A   China
B   Australia
C   Canada
D   Russia

Question 11   Which of the following is a Crown dependency?

A   England
B   Northern Ireland
C   The Channel Islands
D   Scotland

Question 12   Is the statement below TRUE or FALSE?

Dundee and Aberdeen are cities in Northern Ireland

Question 13   Which of the following statements is correct?

A   Big Ben is a popular children's television character
B   Big Ben is the nickname of the great bell in the clock tower of the Houses of Parliament

Question 14   Which of the following statements is correct?

A   A famous sailing event is held at Cowes on the Isle of Wight
B   A famous sailing event is held every year in the city of Belfast

Question 15 Is the statement below TRUE or FALSE?
The UK has a declining elderly population

Question 16 What countries does 'Great Britain' refer to?
A   Just England
B   England, Scotland and Wales
C   England and Scotland
D   England, Scotland and Northern Ireland

Question 17 St Andrew is the patron saint of which country?
A   England
B   Scotland
C   Wales
D   Northern Ireland

Question 18 Which of the following UK landmarks is in Northern Ireland?
A   Big Ben
B   Snowdonia
C   The Giant's Causeway
D   The London Eye

Question 19 Which of the following is a British overseas territory?
A   Northern Ireland
B   The Falkland Islands
C   France
D   USA

Question 20 Which TWO of the following are UK landmarks?
A   The Eisteddfod
B   National Trust
C   Edinburgh Castle
D   The London Eye

British Geography and National Information
Practice Test 2

Question 1 Which of the following statements is correct?

A   National parks are areas of protected countryside that everyone can visit

B   National parks are national sports grounds for people to hold sporting events

Question 2 What is the capital city of Wales?

A   Swansea

B   Cardiff

C   Edinburgh

D   Belfast

Question 3 What task is associated with the National Trust?

A   Conserving native bird species

B   Preserving old aircraft

C   Preserving important buildings and places

D   Looking after classic cars

Question 4 What is the highest-value note issued as British currency?

A   £20

B   £25

C   £50

D   £100

Question 5   Which TWO are famous gardens in the UK?
A   London Eye
B   Sissinghurst
C   Bodnant Garden
D   Snowdonia

Question 6   Is the statement below TRUE or FALSE?
   The daffodil is the national flower of Wales

Question 7   Dunkirk is associated with which TWO events?
A   Landings on D-Day
B   The fall of Singapore
C   The rescue of 300,000 men
D   Small boats coming to the rescue

Question 8   Which is the capital city of the UK?
A   Cardiff
B   Birmingham
C   Manchester
D   London

Question 9   Which of the following statements is correct?
A   The capital cities of the nations of the UK are London, Swansea, Glasgow and Dublin
B   The capital cities of the nations of the UK are London, Cardiff, Edinburgh and Belfast

Question 10   Is the statement below TRUE or FALSE?
   St Helena is a Crown dependency

Question 11   Which TWO of the following are traditional British foods?
A   Strudel
B   Sushi
C   Welsh cakes
D   Haggis

Question 12   What is the title of the UK National Anthem?
A   Long Live the Queen
B   God Save the Queen
C   Long Live the Monarch
D   Almighty is the Queen

Question 13   The Union Flag consists of three crosses. One is St George's.
Who do the other TWO represent?
A   St David
B   St Patrick
C   St Andrew
D   St Piran

Question 14   Is the statement below TRUE or FALSE?
  The Channel Islands are part of the UK

Question 15   Which of the following statements is correct?
A   The capital city of Northern Ireland is Swansea
B   The capital city of Northern Ireland is Belfast

Question 16   Which TWO plants are associated with the UK?
A   Shamrock
B   Rose
C   Cactus
D   Olive tree

Question 17   Which part of the UK is associated with Robert Burns
(1759–96)?
A   England
B   Scotland
C   Wales
D   Ireland

Question 18   Which of the following statements is correct?
A   The capital city of Scotland is Edinburgh
B   The capital city of Scotland is Glasgow

Question **19**   Is the statement below TRUE or FALSE?
The Lake District is England's largest national park

Question **20**   Is the statement below TRUE or FALSE?
The Isle of Man is a Crown dependency

Answers

Practice Test 1: British Geography and National Information

Question 1	A and C		Question 11	C
Question 2	TRUE		Question 12	FALSE
Question 3	B and C		Question 13	B
Question 4	C		Question 14	A
Question 5	C		Question 15	FALSE
Question 6	TRUE		Question 16	B
Question 7	B		Question 17	B
Question 8	TRUE		Question 18	C
Question 9	FALSE		Question 19	B
Question 10	B and C		Question 20	C and D

Practice Test 2: British Geography and National Information

Question 1	A		Question 11	C and D
Question 2	B		Question 12	B
Question 3	C		Question 13	B and C
Question 4	C		Question 14	FALSE
Question 5	B and C		Question 15	B
Question 6	TRUE		Question 16	A and B
Question 7	C and D		Question 17	B
Question 8	D		Question 18	A
Question 9	B		Question 19	TRUE
Question 10	FALSE		Question 20	TRUE

Section 6

Religion, Traditions and Special Dates

	page
Practice Test 1	89
Practice Test 2	93
Answers	97

Religion, Traditions and Special Dates
Practice Test 1

Question 1   What festival is celebrated on 14th February?
A   Valentine's Day
B   Glastonbury
C   Halloween
D   Hogmanay

Question 2   Which of the following statements is correct?
A   Most shops in the UK now open seven days a week
B   All shops in the UK close on Sundays

Question 3   Which TWO of the following are Christian religious festivals celebrated in the UK?
A   Easter
B   Bonfire Night
C   Christmas
D   New Year

Question 4   What event is remembered on 5 November each year?
A   The end of the First World War
B   The Queen's wedding anniversary
C   A plot to blow up the Houses of Parliament in 1605
D   The defeat of the Spanish Armada in 1588

Question 5   Which TWO are Christian groups?
A   Roman Catholics
B   Muslims
C   Hindus
D   Baptists

Question 6   Is the statement below TRUE or FALSE?
In the UK, 1 April is a day when people play jokes on one another

Question 7   Which TWO festivals or traditions are held in November each year?
A   Mother's Day
B   Christmas Day
C   Remembrance Day
D   Bonfire Night

Question 8   Which event occurs each year on the third Sunday in June?
A   Halloween
B   Father's Day
C   Boxing Day
D   Remembrance Day

Question 9   Is the statement below TRUE or FALSE?
In the UK a citizen may only follow a government approved religion

Question 10   Which of the following is a traditional food associated with Scotland?
A   Scones and cream
B   Ulster fry
C   Fish and Chips
D   Haggis

Question 11   Which TWO religions celebrate Diwali?
A   Jews
B   Hindus
C   Christians
D   Sikhs

Question 12   Is the statement below TRUE or FALSE?
In the UK you are expected to respect the rights of others to have their own opinions

Question 13   Which TWO events are religious festivals?
A   Easter
B   Christmas Day
C   New Years Day
D   Glastonbury

Question 14   Which of the following statements is correct?
A   Halloween is a modern American festival that has recently become popular in the UK
B   Halloween has its roots in an ancient pagan festival marking the beginning of winter

Question 15   Is the statement below TRUE or FALSE?
Lent is the period of 40 days before Easter

Question 16   What celebration takes place each year on 25 December?
A   Valentine's Day
B   Christmas Day
C   Halloween
D   Hogmanay

Question 17   Is the statement below TRUE or FALSE?
Getting to know your neighbours can help you to become part of the community

Question 18   Which TWO patron saints' days occur in March?
A   St David
B   St Patrick
C   St George
D   St Andrew

Question 19   On which date is St Patrick's Day celebrated?
A   1 March
B   17 March
C   19 May
D   16 October

Question 20   Which TWO foods are associated with England?

A   Sushi

B   Chicken chow mein

C   Roast beef

D   Fish and chips

Religion, Tradition and Special Dates
Practice Test 2

Question 1   At which festival are mince pies traditionally eaten?
A   The Queen's birthday
B   Glastonbury
C   Christmas
D   Vaisakhi

Question 2   Is the statement below TRUE or FALSE?
A traditional food in Wales is Haggis

Question 3   Which of the following statements is correct?
A   The official Church of state of the UK is the Church of England
B   There is no official Church in the UK

Question 4   Which TWO of the following are traditional British foods?
A   Strudel
B   Sushi
C   Welsh cakes
D   Roast Beef served with vegetables

Question 5   Which of the following statements is correct?
A   Wales and Northern Ireland each have their own Church of state
B   There is no established Church in Wales or Northern Ireland

Question 6   Which of the following statements is correct?
A   Baptists, Methodists and Quakers are all linked to the Roman Catholic Church
B   Baptists, Methodists, and Quakers are Protestant Christian groups

Question 7 Which TWO plants are associated with the UK?
A Shamrock
B Daffodil
C Cactus
D Maple tree

Question 8 During which part of the year are pantomime productions staged in theatres?
A Easter
B Spring
C Christmas
D Summer

Question 9 Which TWO members of a family have a special day dedicated to them?
A Sons
B Fathers
C Mothers
D Cousins

Question 10 What is a bank holiday?
A A public holiday when banks and other businesses close for the day
B A day off for people to set up bank accounts
C A week off for everyone in the UK
D An extra holiday entitlement for working longer hours than usual

Question 11 When is Boxing Day?
A The day after Easter
B The day after Christmas Day
C The last day of the year
D 1 December

Question 12 Which of these is not a Christmas tradition in the UK?
A Giving gifts
B Spending the day on the beach
C Having turkey and vegetables for dinner
D Pulling crackers

Question 13   What is a Yorkshire Pudding?
A   A cake only made in Yorkshire
B   Meat and potato in a pastry
C   Batter cooked in the oven
D   Fruit cake

Question 14   The Archbishop of Canterbury can most accurately be described as what?
A   The spiritual leader of the Church of England
B   The treasurer of the Church of England
C   The administrative leader of the Church of England
D   The political leader of the Church of England

Question 15   The Festival of Lights is another name for which of the following?
A   Christmas
B   Hannukah
C   Diwali
D   Eid ul Adha

Question 16   Which TWO of the following names may be given to the day before Lent starts?
A   Ash Wednesday
B   Shrove Tuesday
C   Easter Sunday
D   Pancake Day

Question 17   Halloween is regarded historically as which of the following?
A   A Christian festival
B   A Muslim festival
C   A Pagan festival
D   A Hindu festival

Question 18   After Protestants, which is the biggest denomination of Christianity in the UK?
A   Jehovah's Witnesses
B   Roman Catholic
C   Ethiopian Orthodox
D   Christian Science

Question 19   Dancing around a maypole, and crowning the queen of May marks which tradition?

A   Bonfire Night
B   Halloween
C   Midsummer
D   May Day

Question 20   On which day do people send cards to someone they admire, anonymously?

A   April Fool's Day
B   New Year's Day
C   Valentine's Day
D   The last day of August

Answers

Practice Test 1: Religion, Traditions and Special Dates

Question 1	A	Question 11	B and D
Question 2	A	Question 12	TRUE
Question 3	A and C	Question 13	A and B
Question 4	C	Question 14	B
Question 5	A and D	Question 15	TRUE
Question 6	TRUE	Question 16	B
Question 7	C and D	Question 17	TRUE
Question 8	B	Question 18	A and B
Question 9	FALSE	Question 19	B
Question 10	D	Question 20	C and D

Practice Test 2: Religion, Traditions and Special Dates

Question 1	C	Question 11	B
Question 2	FALSE	Question 12	B
Question 3	A	Question 13	C
Question 4	C and D	Question 14	A
Question 5	B	Question 15	C
Question 6	B	Question 16	B and D
Question 7	A and B	Question 17	C
Question 8	C	Question 18	B
Question 9	B and C	Question 19	D
Question 10	A	Question 20	C

CPSIA information can be obtained
at www.ICGtesting.com
Printed in the USA
LVHW061948220622
721699LV00008B/264

9 781789 633337